Ghosts of the Stage: Ten Hauntings at the Theatre

While every precaution has been taken in the preparation of this book, the publisher assumes no responsibility for errors or omissions, or for damages resulting from the use of the information contained herein.

GHOSTS OF THE STAGE: TEN HAUNTINGS AT THE THEATRE

First edition. July 8, 2023.

ISBN: 979-8223737377

Written by Edward Turner.

Also by Edward Turner

Ghosts of Paris: Ten Haunted Places in the City of Love
Appalachian Nightmares: The Top 10 Creepy Creatures of the Mountains
Asia's Top Ten Cryptids: Legends, Sightings, and Theories
Beyond the Shadows: Unlocking the Mystery of Bigfoot
Evil Women in History: Uncovering the Gruesome Crimes of Ten Notorious Female Killers
Ghosts of London: Ten Haunted Places in The City
Ghosts of New York: Ten Haunted Places in The Big Apple
Ghosts of Oregon: The Top 10 Haunted Places You Must Visit
Ghosts of the Stage: Ten Hauntings at the Theatre
Missouri Nightmares: The Top 10 Chilling Legends
Mothman Unleashed: Into the Darkened Skies
North America's Top Ten Cryptids: Legends, Sightings, and Theories
Philly's Phantom Encounters: Exploring the City's Most Haunted Places
Secrets of the Deep: The Mystery of the Loch Ness Monster
Unsolved Mysteries: Delving into the Shadows of Infamous Murders and Enigmatic Killers
Unveiling the Shadows: A Journey into Financial Crimes and Scandals

Introduction

The Enthralling Allure of Haunted Theaters

From the eerie silence of an empty stage to the rustling whispers of velvet curtains, there's something intrinsically captivating about theatres. Yet, when shadows of the past linger, manifesting as unexplained whispers and spectral appearances, the allure becomes even more profound. The haunted theatre has become a staple in our collective psyche, a blend of our fascination with the supernatural and the historical significance of these grand establishments.

Why do haunted theatres captivate us so intensely? Perhaps it is the confluence of the ephemeral and the enduring, the spectral and the real. Theatres, in their essence, are places of stories. Countless tales have been spun on their stages, each performance adding another layer to their intricate tapestry of human emotion. The palpable presence of past performances, echoed in the aged wood and worn velvet, provides a tangible link to bygone eras. This powerful sense of history makes it easy for us to imagine unseen spectres, still yearning to perform their final curtain call.

Haunted theatres also play on our innate curiosity about the afterlife. Despite our advances in science and technology, death remains a mystery. This unknown naturally breeds stories, myths, and legends. The haunted theatre, thus, provides a comfortable stage where this fascination can play out, where the line between life and death, reality and fantasy, is thrillingly blurred. The creak of a seat in an empty auditorium, the inexplicable chill in a spotlight's glow, the uncanny echo of an actor's line; these become signs of a spectral presence, enticing our curiosity and challenging our perception of reality.

Our fascination with haunted theatres is also rooted in their intrinsic historical significance. The theatres included in this book have been meticulously selected for their rich cultural heritage and unique historical importance. These are places that have witnessed significant events, welcomed famed performers, and played pivotal roles in shaping society and the arts. From the baroque grandeur of old European opera houses to the gilded decadence of Broadway's early days, these theatres are landmarks of cultural evolution. The hauntings associated with them only add to their allure, intertwining the spectral with the historical, crafting narratives that are as spine-chilling as they are captivating.

These theatres have been chosen not only for the authenticity of their hauntings but also for what they represent in their respective societies. Each haunting speaks to its cultural context, reflecting societal beliefs and fears about death, the afterlife, and the supernatural. The ghosts of these theatres, whether they are mourning lovers, vengeful performers, or tragic figures, offer intriguing glimpses into the societies they originate from, making their stories all the more compelling.

GHOSTS OF THE STAGE: TEN HAUNTINGS AT THE THEATRE

In "Ghosts of the Stage: Ten Hauntings at the Theater", we explore these hauntingly beautiful architectural marvels, traversing through time and space, history and mystery. We delve into their spectral stories, examine their historical significance, and ponder their cultural implications. As we lift the curtain on these theatres' haunted histories, we invite you to suspend disbelief, to listen for the whispers in the wings, and to join us in exploring the captivating allure of these haunted stages.

Chapter 1: The New Amsterdam Theater in New York, New York

—

History, Hauntings, and Hypotheses

In the heart of New York City, the New Amsterdam Theater stands as a testament to the timeless glamour of Broadway. Opened in 1903, it has seen over a century of history, its rich past woven from a colourful tapestry of performances, personalities, and, of course, phantoms. Drawing on historical archives, local legends, and first hand interviews, we delve into the intriguing story of this theatre and its famed spectre, a Ziegfeld Follies showgirl known as Olive Thomas.

Historical archives paint a vivid picture of New Amsterdam's past. It was a shining star in the early 20th century, a jewel in the crown of Broadway, hosting illustrious performers and glamorous productions. The Ziegfeld Follies, a series of extravagant theatrical revues, was one of the theatre's most successful runs. Olive Thomas, one of its brightest stars, tragically passed away under mysterious circumstances during the show's height, and it is her spirit that purportedly haunts the theatre.

Local legends and firsthand interviews bring Olive's spectral presence to life. Many staff members have reported sightings of a beautiful woman in a beaded dress and a green sash, Olive's signature look. They describe the scent of vintage perfume wafting through the air and faint strains of old show tunes echoing in the otherwise silent theatre. Most notably, Olive's spirit seems harmless, often appearing to be lost or in search of something.

Despite the consistent sightings and eerie experiences, some sceptics have sought to explain the New Amsterdam's haunting through scientific and natural theories. Psychologists argue that our brains are pattern-seeking machines, prone to attributing human characteristics to random occurrences - a phenomenon known as pareidolia. For example, a sudden chill could be ascribed to a ghostly presence, when it could be simply a draft.

Infrasound, sound waves with frequencies below the lower limit of human audibility, have also been offered as an explanation. In certain circumstances, infrasound can cause feelings of uneasiness and chills, potentially explaining the 'supernatural' sensations reported.

Moreover, the power of suggestion and the influence of the theatre's history could contribute to the spectral sightings. If a person is aware of Olive's story and the accounts of her apparition, they might be more likely to interpret ambiguous situations as ghostly encounters.

However, these scientific explanations often fall short of fully explaining the peculiar happenings at the New Amsterdam Theater. For instance, they don't explain the simultaneous sightings of Olive by multiple people or the specific details of her appearance matching historical records.

Whether one attributes the strange occurrences to the supernatural or seeks solace in science, the story of the New Amsterdam Theater remains a captivating blend of history, legend, and mystery. It's a narrative that continues to evolve, an enduring testament to Broadway's glamorous past and its spectral inhabitants.

Architectural Allure of the New Amsterdam Theater

AS WE FURTHER EXPLORE the New Amsterdam Theater, its grand architecture and design elements deserve special attention. For not only do they contribute to the theatre's majestic aesthetic and mystique, but they might also hold keys to the scientific explanations of the paranormal phenomena reported within its hallowed halls.

The New Amsterdam Theater, designed by architects Herts and Tallant, is a stunning example of the Art Nouveau style. Its facade, embellished with intricate floral motifs, delicate ironwork, and sinuous lines, beckons theatre-goers into a world that harks back to a time of glamour and sophistication. Inside, the theatre continues to impress with its opulent decorations, stucco mouldings, and beautiful murals.

These exquisite design elements, coupled with the theatre's rich history, imbue the building with a mystique that's hard to resist. The walls, embellished with patterns and scenes from ages past, seem to hum with stories untold, the grand stage a silent witness to a century of laughter, tears, drama, and spectacle. This potent sense of history and the sheer beauty of the theatre's design play into our innate human love for stories and our fascination with the past, stirring our imaginations and fueling the spectral folklore.

From a scientific perspective, the architectural features could indeed contribute to the theatre's paranormal reputation. For instance, the ornate decorations and grand chandeliers could create unusual shadows and light play, which, in the dimmed theatre lighting, could be misinterpreted as spectral figures or movements. Sound is another factor worth considering. The domed ceiling and cavernous auditorium are perfect for amplifying and distorting sounds. A soft whisper from the wings could turn into a spectral murmur by the time it reaches the back rows.

Furthermore, the structure of the building itself can cause unusual drafts and temperature fluctuations. Old buildings, such as the New Amsterdam Theater, often have hidden vents, irregular insulation, and extensive networks of passages, which can cause sudden gusts of wind or areas of cold air. These natural phenomena, when experienced in the context of a theatre renowned for its hauntings, could be easily misconstrued as paranormal activity.

The theatre's architecture, in essence, creates a 'haunted house' effect. The beautiful but slightly decayed grandeur, the play of light and shadow, the echoing sounds, and the unexplained drafts all contribute to a heightened sense of the eerie, enhancing the overall mystique of the theatre.

GHOSTS OF THE STAGE: TEN HAUNTINGS AT THE THEATRE

In sum, the New Amsterdam Theater stands as a beautiful confluence of art, history, and mystery. Its architecture and design, majestic and slightly eerie, both shape and reflect the theatre's intriguing narrative. Whether it's the final bow of a spectral showgirl or the whisper of history echoing through its grand auditorium, the theatre continues to captivate, its stories, both seen and unseen, forever embedded in its walls.

Chapter 2: The Oregon Shakespeare Festival in Ashland, Oregon

The Play's the Thing, Wherein We'll Catch the Ghosts of Theaters Past

Situated in the heart of Ashland, Oregon, the Oregon Shakespeare Festival (OSF) is a theatrical institution that dates back to 1935. Under the visionary direction of Angus Bowmer, what began as a modest two-play festival held in a borrowed boxing ring has evolved into one of the oldest and largest professional non-profit theatres in the United States. Each year, the OSF stages a series of plays that run the gamut from the works of its namesake, Shakespeare, to contemporary and classic pieces, all in repertory.

The OSF's history is characterised by its determined spirit. After the original outdoor Elizabethan stage, essentially a makeshift structure with a proscenium arch and Elizabethan half-timbered façade, was demolished in the 1940s, it was replaced in 1959 by a dedicated open-air theatre that drew inspiration from London's 1599 Fortune Theatre. The indoor Angus Bowmer Theatre and the smaller, more contemporary Thomas Theatre completed the ensemble of stages, each with its distinct architectural charm and each, according to reports, with its own spectral residents.

Over the years, countless tales of otherworldly presences have emerged from the OSF's theatres. Actors, technicians, and staff members have reported uncanny experiences, from eerie sensations to apparitions, particularly during late-night rehearsals and performances. The spirits are rumoured to be particularly fond of Shakespeare's works, often making their presence known during performances of tragedies like "Macbeth" and "Hamlet."

At the heart of the OSF's spectral folklore is the ghost of Richard L. Hay, a prominent designer at the festival for over 50 years. Hay, who passed away in 2011, had a profound impact on the OSF, designing the two main theatres and contributing significantly to its growth and reputation. Staff members have reported seeing his apparition in the theatre, usually during technical difficulties. It's as if he continues to watch over the festival, offering spectral assistance and ensuring the quality of the productions.

Another frequent spectral visitor is thought to be the spirit of an actor who fell from the outdoor Elizabethan stage during a performance of "Henry V" in the late 1940s. Stories abound of eerie echoes of his lines and a figure seen falling from the stage late at night.

These ghost stories align intriguingly with the historical context of the theatre and region. Ashland, like many old towns, has its share of ghostly tales that reflect its rich past of Native American heritage, pioneering settlements, and gold rush booms. The OSF ghost stories seem to mirror this tradition, weaving historical figures and events into the supernatural narratives. This synchrony of theatre and regional folklore reflects the OSF's deep-rooted connection with the community, reinforcing its cultural significance and enriching its spectral allure.

Moreover, the ghosts of OSF seem to embody the theatre's essence. Just as the festival honours the past while continuously evolving, its spectral inhabitants represent figures from its history, their narratives evolving with each new sighting. In a way, they are the ultimate tribute to the power of theatre, testifying to the enduring impact of the artists who've graced its stages.

The Oregon Shakespeare Festival, with its grand history and spectral tales, remains a testament to the enduring power of theatre. It offers a stage where past and present intermingle, where history is retold, and where the boundary between the real and the supernatural blurs into an intriguing performance of life, death, and everything in between.

The Plays and Paranormal Phenomena at the Oregon Shakespeare Festival

IT'S A LONG-STANDING tradition in theatre that certain plays, especially those by Shakespeare, carry a supernatural weight. "Macbeth," for instance, is famously regarded as cursed, its very name often avoided in theatrical circles and replaced by the euphemistic "The Scottish Play." At the Oregon Shakespeare Festival (OSF), the repertoire's relationship with the reported hauntings offers a captivating study of how the thematic content and emotions of productions might influence experiences of the supernatural.

One notable correlation arises with the staging of Shakespeare's tragedies. Reports of ghostly activity appear to spike during the production of plays like "Macbeth," "Hamlet," and "King Lear," all of which delve into the darker aspects of human nature and the supernatural. Could it be that the intense emotions and themes explored in these plays create an environment conducive to experiences of the otherworldly? Or perhaps these productions, with their existential themes and spectral characters, make those involved more receptive to the idea of encountering spirits.

The ghost of Richard L. Hay, the renowned OSF designer, also exhibits a fascinating connection with the festival's repertoire. Accounts suggest that his apparition appears most frequently during technical rehearsals, often when the crew is grappling with a particularly challenging set or lighting design. It's almost as if the aesthetic of the production, a domain Hay had mastered during his lifetime, draws his spirit back to the theatre.

Moreover, the tragic tale of the actor who fell from the Elizabethan stage during a performance of "Henry V" intertwines with the theatre's productions in a poignant way. Witnesses report hearing ghostly echoes of his lines or seeing his spectral figure falling from the stage, particularly during the staging of historical plays or dramas with tragic endings.

These correlations suggest a compelling hypothesis - the theatrical environment, charged with the energy of dramatic narratives and heightened emotions, could make people more attuned to paranormal experiences. The intensity of the performances, the darkness of the theatre, and the thematic exploration of mortality, betrayal, and the supernatural might create a psychological and emotional space where the boundaries between reality and the otherworldly become porous.

Scientifically, this could be explained through a psychological phenomenon known as priming. If an individual is repeatedly exposed to specific stimuli (in this case, the themes of death, ghosts, and the supernatural in the plays), they become 'primed' to perceive related concepts more readily. This means that a person working on a ghost-themed play might be more likely to interpret ambiguous stimuli, such as an unexpected gust of wind or a strange shadow, as paranormal activity.

However, this doesn't diminish the allure or validity of the reported hauntings. Whether they're psychological phenomena or genuine spectral appearances, they add another fascinating layer to the Oregon Shakespeare Festival's rich tapestry, creating a theatre experience where life, art, and the afterlife engagingly converge.

16

Chapter 3: Le Petit Theatre in New Orleans, Louisiana

A Stage for Specters in the Heart of New Orleans

Situated in the heart of New Orleans' French Quarter, Le Petit Théâtre du Vieux Carre, fondly known as Le Petit Theatre, is a cultural icon. With its history dating back to 1916, this playhouse's storied past is as vibrant as the city itself, intertwining historical events, colourful characters, and an enticing undercurrent of the supernatural.

New Orleans, a city steeped in history, culture, and a deep-rooted belief in the supernatural, provides a captivating backdrop for Le Petit Theatre's ghostly tales. Renowned for its tales of voodoo, haunted plantations, and spectral presences, the city's folklore forms an intricate tapestry of the supernatural that seems to extend into the very fabric of the theatre.

The primary spectral resident of Le Petit Theatre is believed to be the ghost of a priest. According to local accounts, this spiritual entity, affectionately dubbed Pere Dagobert, is most frequently seen or heard during rehearsals. Reports describe hearing melodic chanting, akin to the hymns sung during Mass, emanating from the wings when the theatre is otherwise silent.

Historical records provide a fascinating context for these spectral encounters. In the late 18th century, much before the theatre came into existence, the land was home to St. Peter's Church. Pere Antoine, a revered Capuchin monk, led the church. Legend has it that Pere Antoine continues his divine duties in death, offering comfort and guidance, his presence manifesting in the theatre that now stands on his erstwhile parish grounds.

Furthermore, there have been numerous reports of the theatre's seats inexplicably flipping down, as if an unseen audience is taking their places. Witnesses have also observed a ghostly woman dressed in antebellum attire, looking as though she's eagerly awaiting a performance. These occurrences, interwoven with the theatre's function and history, add to its spectral narrative and reflect the city's folklore, where spirits often mirror the roles they played in life.

The rich folklore of New Orleans also intersects intriguingly with Le Petit Theatre's hauntings. In local culture, spirits are often seen as guides or protectors, their existence viewed as an extension of the city's living history. Similarly, the ghostly inhabitants of Le Petit Theatre appear to be benign, their presence adding to the theatre's unique charm rather than causing alarm.

Moreover, the ghost stories of Le Petit Theatre share another common thread with New Orleans folklore - they serve as an affirmation of the city's past. Just as the city's spectral legends often recall historical events or figures, the theatre's ghost stories are closely tied to its history. They keep alive the narratives of individuals who once graced the theatre, whether as priests offering spiritual guidance or patrons seeking entertainment, thus ensuring that their stories remain an integral part of its present.

The haunted history of Le Petit Théâtre du Vieux Carre beautifully encapsulates the allure of New Orleans - a city where history, culture, and the supernatural dance a perpetual waltz. The theatre, with its living legacy and spectral tales, remains a captivating stage where the dramas of life and afterlife are equally celebrated.

A Cultural Intersection

NEW ORLEANS, THE EFFERVESCENT heart of Louisiana, is a city rich with a diverse cultural tapestry woven from threads of French, African, Spanish, and Native American heritage. This eclectic mix lends the city a unique cultural context, particularly evident in its supernatural folklore. The city's stories of voodoo, ghosts, and haunted locales are not mere tourist attractions but rather integral aspects of its cultural identity. This cultural context provides a fascinating lens through which to examine the hauntings reported at Le Petit Theatre.

To comprehend the intersection of New Orleans' supernatural folklore and Le Petit Theatre's hauntings, one must first understand the city's unique perspective on death and the afterlife. New Orleans, with its vibrant Mardi Gras and jazz funerals, embraces death not as an end but a transition to another stage of existence. This view imbues the city's folklore with a sense of familiarity rather than fear towards the supernatural.

In the case of Le Petit Theatre, its benign hauntings reflect this cultural perspective. The ghostly sightings reported at the theatre are not menacing but rather peaceful, almost as though the spirits consider the theatre as their home. The apparition of Pere Dagobert, in particular, resonates with the city's view of spirits as protectors or guides. His ethereal chanting is seen as a comforting presence, reflecting the narrative of helpful entities found in many New Orleans ghost stories.

New Orleans' cultural context also includes a strong sense of community and history. Stories, music, and rituals are tools to keep the past alive and celebrate the city's history. This cultural tradition is echoed in the hauntings of Le Petit Theatre. The spectral inhabitants of the theatre often seem to be enacting the roles they held in life, their ghostly narratives intricately linked with the theatre's and the city's past. Their continued presence ensures that the history they represent remains a vibrant part of the theatre's narrative.

Moreover, the city's folklore is steeped in the mystical traditions of voodoo, a belief system that coexists with more mainstream religious practices. It underscores the idea of spirits interacting with the living world, further influencing how locals perceive the hauntings. While there haven't been reports of voodoo-related phenomena at Le Petit Theatre, the openness towards the supernatural ingrained in the city's culture likely contributes to the acceptance and preservation of the theatre's spectral tales.

Finally, New Orleans is a city of stories and storytelling is at the heart of theatre. The ghostly apparitions of Le Petit Theatre enrich this tradition, their tales enhancing the drama both on and off-stage. Just as the city's folklore comprises engaging narratives passed down generations, the theatre's hauntings form an ongoing ghostly drama that adds another dimension to its cultural significance.

In essence, the cultural context of New Orleans' supernatural folklore and the reported hauntings at Le Petit Theatre intersect at multiple levels, enhancing each other in a vibrant dance of life, death, and drama. It's a testament to the city's rich culture, where the living history and the afterlife share a stage, adding to the enigmatic allure of Le Petit Theatre.

EDWARD TURNER

Chapter 4: The Variety Theater in Cleveland, Ohio

An Ode to the Paranormal

The Variety Theatre, situated in Cleveland, Ohio, is a relic of grandeur frozen in time. Since its opening in 1927, the theatre has seen a myriad of transformations, from a Vaudeville house to a cinema, and eventually to a concert venue, hosting legendary acts like The Doors and AC/DC. Today, though it stands mostly dormant, it continues to put on a different kind of show—one that entrances paranormal enthusiasts.

Numerous accounts of spectral sightings, mysterious sounds, and eerie feelings of being watched have been reported at the Variety Theatre. Based on interviews with former employees, theatregoers, and local investigators, and supplemented with primary sources like newspaper clippings and historical records, a captivating portrait of the theatre's haunted history emerges.

Many witnesses describe encounters with a spectral figure believed to be Fritz, a former manager of the theatre. Fritz's apparition, clad in period attire, has been spotted in the theatre's lobby and office area. He appears so real that he's often mistaken for a living person—until he vanishes into thin air. Accounts suggest that Fritz is a benign entity, seeming to carry on with his managerial duties, perhaps unaware that he's no longer among the living.

But not all apparitions at the Variety Theatre are as gentle as Fritz. Some reports detail unnerving encounters with a malevolent entity in the basement. Witnesses describe an oppressive atmosphere, a feeling of intense fear, and even physical symptoms like scratches or unexplained bruises after visiting the area. One chilling account from a former janitor recounts how he found all the chairs in the basement stacked in a pyramid overnight—a feat impossible for a human to accomplish single-handedly in such a short span of time.

These paranormal occurrences at the Variety Theatre are intriguingly linked with its history. The theatre has had its share of misfortune and tragedy, including a deadly fire and the unsolved murder of a young actress in the 1940s. It's been suggested that these dark chapters could have left an indelible mark on the theatre, resulting in the residual hauntings.

The figure of Fritz, for instance, may be a manifestation of the theatre's happier times, an echo of the past when Variety Theatre was a bustling hub of entertainment. His apparition, along with the reports of phantom applause and music heard in the main auditorium, seems to reflect the theatre's vibrant history.

On the other hand, the malevolent entity in the basement could be connected to the theatre's tragic events. While it's challenging to definitively tie this entity to a specific event, the intense fear and negativity associated with it suggest a link with the theatre's darker past. It's possible that this entity represents the anguish and trauma associated with these tragedies, its presence a stark contrast to the benign hauntings in other areas of the theatre.

The Variety Theatre serves as a fascinating study of the interplay between history and the paranormal. It stands as a testament to the past, its spectral occurrences a reminder of its glorious and grim chapters. The theatre, in its silence, continues to tell its stories, blurring the line between the living history and the afterlife in its captivating paranormal performance.

A Spectral Timeline

THE TIMELINE OF PARANORMAL activity at the Variety Theatre offers an intriguing correlation with certain historical events and societal changes. A closer examination of these overlapping periods reveals a potential link between external circumstances and the reported supernatural occurrences.

One of the peak periods of reported paranormal activity at the Variety Theatre coincides with the late 1960s and early 1970s, a tumultuous era characterised by the Civil Rights Movement, anti-Vietnam War protests, and a significant cultural shift. Interestingly, it was during this period that the theatre transitioned from a movie cinema to a rock concert venue, featuring rebellious, groundbreaking bands of the time.

The heightened societal tension and the cultural revolution of this era seemed to mirror the increased paranormal activity within the Variety Theatre. Many witnesses reported an intensification in Fritz's apparitions, as though the theatre's transition and the societal upheaval had stirred him. Could it be that the shift in the theatre's cultural role, paralleling the societal changes, disturbed the spiritual energy within the building?

Moreover, accounts of the malevolent entity in the basement became more frequent and intense during the late 1980s and early 1990s, a period marked by economic recession, increased crime rates, and societal unease. Could this negative entity have been a manifestation or amplifier of the external societal discord? The entity's increased aggression during this time suggests a potential connection.

On a local level, one notable peak in paranormal activity occurred around the time of the theatre's near-demolition in the mid-2000s. The threat to the theatre's existence seemed to evoke a surge in spectral sightings and uncanny events. The apparition of Fritz was reportedly seen more frequently, and even more intriguingly, a group of spectral theatregoers was observed, seemingly awaiting a show that would never start.

The possible link between the theatre's spectral timeline and historical events brings us to a captivating hypothesis. Could significant societal changes and local events imbue a location with emotional energy, contributing to paranormal activity? While this link is largely speculative and not scientifically proven, it adds a fascinating layer to the understanding of the theatre's hauntings. It suggests that the theatre, as a historical entity, may not only record its own history but also reflect the broader societal narrative.

The Variety Theatre presents an enticing dance between the material and the spectral, the historical and the uncanny. Its walls seem to echo not only its own past but the world's evolving story, resonating in an ongoing spectral performance. As the theatre continues to stand against time, it remains a silent yet powerful narrator, its paranormal tales a captivating blend of history and mystery.

EDWARD TURNER

Chapter 5: The Kalamazoo Civic Theater in Kalamazoo, Michigan

An Encore of the Ethereal

Nestled in the heart of Michigan, the Kalamazoo Civic Theatre, since its opening in 1929, has been an emblem of artistic brilliance, fostering local talent and hosting a variety of performances. However, beyond its renown as a beacon of the arts, the theatre is also famed for its spectral inhabitants, an intriguing facet that weaves together actors, staff, and patrons in a narrative beyond the ordinary.

From firsthand accounts of actors and staff, a compelling picture of the theatre's ghostly phenomena takes shape. Actors, practising their lines on an empty stage, often speak of an unseen audience, their murmurs rustling in the auditorium like ghostly applause. Staff members recount eerie experiences of footsteps echoing in deserted corridors, and whispers seeping through the walls when silence should reign.

One of the most frequently reported apparitions is that of a ghostly woman in white, affectionately referred to as "Thelma." Said to be a friendly presence, Thelma is often seen watching rehearsals from the balcony, her spectral form visible out of the corner of one's eye. She is also known to fiddle with lighting equipment, her playful antics seen as encouragement rather than a nuisance.

To understand the theatre's haunted reputation, we must delve into its historical and cultural context. The Kalamazoo Civic Theatre was born from the passion of civic leaders, including the philanthropist W.E. Upjohn. It was his niece, Thelma Mertz, who became the theatre's first managing director. Thelma, known for her love for the theatre and commitment to the arts, tragically passed away in an automobile accident in 1932. It is believed by many that her spirit continues to inhabit the theatre, the ethereal lady in white a spectral reminder of her undying love for the stage.

Furthermore, the theatre's construction coincided with the period of the Great Depression. The economic turmoil and societal hardships of the time were profound, leaving a lasting emotional imprint. It's possible that the theatre, a place of solace during these challenging times, absorbed some of this emotional energy, contributing to the reported paranormal phenomena.

The cultural factors surrounding the Kalamazoo Civic Theatre also provide insight into its haunted reputation. Theatres, in general, are steeped in superstitions, from the curse of "Macbeth" to the tradition of leaving a "ghost light" on stage after a performance. This cultural context, coupled with the theatre's own history, might contribute to the heightened awareness of the supernatural among its occupants.

Additionally, Kalamazoo is a city rich in Native American history. Some theories suggest that the land on which the theatre was built may have been significant to indigenous tribes, and the spiritual energy associated with the area could be a factor in the reported hauntings.

The Kalamazoo Civic Theatre offers a mesmerising blend of history, culture, and the supernatural. Its spectral tales continue to be an integral part of its identity, adding a layer of mystique to the venue. The theatre, in its grandeur and spectral charm, continues to fascinate, providing not only a stage for the living but also a home for the spirits that refuse to bow out.

A Shadow on the Stage

IN ANY NARRATIVE, BE it of a person or a place, there are chapters of joy and chapters of sorrow. The story of the Kalamazoo Civic Theatre is no different. Amidst its tale of artistry and culture, a page is turned to a tragedy that casts a shadow over the theatre, influencing not only its spectral reputation but also the perception of its local residents.

The tragedy in question unfolded in the winter of 1932 when Thelma Mertz, the theatre's beloved first managing director, met an untimely demise in a catastrophic automobile accident. Thelma, niece of the philanthropist W.E. Upjohn, a passionate theatre enthusiast, was deeply admired for her commitment to the arts. Her loss, coming just three years after the theatre's opening, sent ripples of sorrow through the community.

Thelma's death had a profound impact on the perception of the Kalamazoo Civic Theatre. To the local residents, the theatre wasn't merely a building, but a community endeavour, a symbol of their collective pride. Thelma, through her role as managing director, was intimately linked to this symbol. Her abrupt departure seemed to cast a pall of sadness over the theatre, transforming it from a beacon of joy to a reminder of loss.

In the aftermath of Thelma's death, rumours began to circulate about her spirit haunting the theatre. The sightings of a spectral woman in white watching rehearsals from the balcony, adjusting lighting equipment, and causing a general friendly fuss, were attributed to Thelma's ghost. The local community, many of whom had personally known Thelma, began to perceive the theatre not only as a cultural hub but also as the eternal home of a loved one.

This perception had a significant impact on the theatre's reputation. It became a site of fascination for those interested in the paranormal, its allure transcending the local community to attract ghost hunters and paranormal researchers. However, it also deepened the emotional connection between the theatre and its patrons. They saw the ghostly tales not as mere scary stories but as an enduring testament to Thelma's love for the theatre and the arts.

While the tragedy undoubtedly cast a shadow over the theatre, it also gave it a unique character. Thelma's spectral presence humanised the grand edifice, offering a comforting narrative of love outlasting death. The theatre became a tangible link between the world of the living and the world of spirits, its stage hosting a continuous performance of history, culture, and mystery.

To this day, the Kalamazoo Civic Theatre's haunted reputation continues to be a part of its charm. The shadow of the tragedy has long since blended with the theatre's overall narrative, painting a picture that is as poignant as it is intriguing. The theatre, in all its spectral grandeur, stands as a testament to the

enduring bond between a community and its cultural landmark,
a bond that transcends even death.

EDWARD TURNER

Chapter 6: The Theatre Royal, Drury Lane in London, England

A Stage for Spectres

The Theatre Royal, Drury Lane, holds the title of London's oldest theatre, its foundation laid in 1663. Within its storied walls, the theatre holds more than three centuries of dramatic history, and according to countless testimonies and tales, a spectral cast that refuses to leave the stage.

Several infamous ghost stories swirl around this venerable institution, their spectral characters woven into the theatre's rich tapestry. Corroborated by historical records, eyewitness testimonies, and countless retellings, these ghostly narratives add an ethereal dimension to the theatre's past.

Perhaps the most famous of the Theatre Royal's supernatural residents is the "Man in Grey." This ghostly figure, often seen in a powdered wig, tricorn hat, and riding cloak, is typically spotted in the Upper Circle, usually during the day. Strangely, his appearances have been linked to successful runs of plays, leading many to consider him a good omen. The Man in Grey is believed to be the ghost of a man whose skeletal remains were discovered within a walled-up side passage in the theatre during renovations in the early 19th century. In his pocket was a dagger, suggesting a violent end that might explain his eternal residence.

The spectral figure of the legendary clown Joseph Grimaldi is another fascinating presence. Grimaldi, who essentially defined the traditional character of the pantomime clown, has been reported to aid actors in their performances, literally guiding them around the stage. Historical records confirm Grimaldi's deep love for the theatre and his craft, offering some context to his posthumous stage directions.

Another chilling tale revolves around the ghost of Charles Macklin. An actor at the Theatre Royal in the 18th century, Macklin had a notorious temper. In a fit of rage, he murdered a fellow actor, Thomas Hallam, by driving a cane into his eye. Macklin's spirit is said to roam the theatre, particularly near the spot of his dreadful crime, filling the air with an unnerving chill.

The theatre's long and varied past provides fertile ground for these spectral narratives. Its history is a tapestry of triumphs, failures, controversies, and tragedies, each leaving an emotional imprint on the building. Over the centuries, the Theatre Royal has seen fires and rebuildings, changes in management, and shifts in society's tastes, all while witnessing the ebb and flow of countless lives within its walls.

Historically, theatres are spaces of heightened emotions, from the ecstasy of a triumphant performance to the despair of a play falling flat. These intense emotions could potentially imprint themselves on the fabric of the place, creating "recordings" that replay under certain conditions, which might explain some of the ghostly phenomena reported.

Culturally, ghost stories are integral to theatre lore. The very act of storytelling is a means of connecting with the past, and what better way to do so than through tales that bring history to life, albeit of a spectral nature. The infamous ghost stories of the Theatre Royal, Drury Lane, serve to deepen the historical richness of the theatre, adding an allure that makes it as fascinating to ghost hunters as it is to theatre enthusiasts.

The Theatre Royal, Drury Lane, stands as a magnificent monument to theatrical history, its ghostly tales a spectral echo of its rich past. The narratives of the Man in Grey, Joseph Grimaldi, and Charles Macklin intertwine history with mystery, their ghostly footprints a fascinating testament to the theatre's enduring appeal.

The Literary Connection at Theatre Royal, Drury Lane

DRAMA AND THE SUPERNATURAL have long been intertwined. At their core, both seek to explore the human condition, albeit in different dimensions. In the context of the Theatre Royal, Drury Lane, this connection takes on a tangible form. The rich tapestry of literature and drama performed at the theatre intersects intriguingly with its spectral narratives, contributing to its supernatural reputation.

Throughout its history, the Theatre Royal, Drury Lane has been a premier venue for both classic and contemporary productions. Its stages have seen a myriad of themes, from the depths of human despair to the heights of divine comedy. These themes often resonate with the theatre's ghostly tales, the line between fiction and spectral reality seemingly blurred.

One clear connection is the theatre's association with the works of William Shakespeare. The Bard's plays, known for their exploration of the human condition, often include elements of the supernatural. Ghostly apparitions, prophecies, and omens are common plot devices in plays like Macbeth, Hamlet, and Julius Caesar. Performing these plays in a theatre reputedly inhabited by spirits adds an eerie authenticity to the productions, further entrenching the theatre's supernatural reputation.

The infamous ghost of Charles Macklin, known for his violent temper and the murder of a fellow actor, resonates with themes of rage and revenge found in many tragedies performed on the Drury Lane stage. The narrative of Macklin's restless spirit, forever roaming the scene of his crime, parallels the tragic trajectory of characters who let their unchecked emotions lead them to their downfall.

Similarly, the ghostly presence of Joseph Grimaldi, the legendary clown, connects with the often tragic figures of jesters, fools, and clowns in drama. The tales of his spectral guidance to actors mirrors the role of these characters in literature, providing insight and direction amidst chaos and confusion. Grimaldi's posthumous performances serve as a poignant reminder of the theatre's commitment to its art, the lines between life and drama blurred in spectral continuity.

GHOSTS OF THE STAGE: TEN HAUNTINGS AT THE THEATRE

Moreover, the theatre's performance of Gothic literature, known for its blend of horror, romance, and the supernatural, further contributes to its spectral reputation. The ethereal themes of these narratives, coupled with the theatre's ghostly tales, create an immersive experience for the audience, enhancing the allure of the supernatural.

Finally, the hauntingly beautiful performance of operas and ballets, often fraught with themes of love, loss, and tragedy, could potentially stir up the theatre's spectral residents. The heightened emotions elicited during these performances might resonate with the spirits, leading to increased paranormal activity.

The literature and drama performed at the Theatre Royal, Drury Lane, play a significant role in its supernatural reputation. The thematic connections between the stage productions and the theatre's ghostly stories provide a fascinating backdrop that enhances the theatre's spectral charm. As the curtain rises for each performance, the line between the world of drama and the spectral realm seems to fade, leaving behind a stage where both the living and the dead have a role to play.

EDWARD TURNER

Chapter 7: The Huguan Huiguan Opera House in Beijing, China

Echoes of Folklore and History

Nestled in the bustling heart of Beijing, China, the Huguan Huiguan Opera House stands as a unique testament to the country's rich blend of folklore, history, and theatre. Often overlooked by tourists, this unassuming structure houses centuries of art and legend, including an array of ghostly tales that colour its rich narrative.

From its construction in the Ming Dynasty (1368–1644), the Opera House has served as a hub for Chinese operatic arts, its stage hosting countless performances that have captured the hearts of audiences for generations. However, its long history has also borne witness to moments of turmoil and heartache, which have given birth to tales of spectral inhabitants that reportedly haunt its premises.

Among the myriad ghost stories associated with the Huguan Huiguan Opera House, one tale stands out. The tragic figure of a young opera actress, who took her own life due to a forbidden love affair, is said to haunt the dressing rooms and backstage areas. This heartbreaking tale mirrors many of the narratives performed on stage, often centred around star-crossed lovers and tragic endings, thereby potentially creating a resonance between life and art.

Historically, Chinese society places great emphasis on societal norms and family honour, concepts that are often reflected in its literature and drama. The story of the young actress's forbidden love and subsequent suicide mirrors these themes, and her spirit's reported lingering presence serves as a chilling reminder of the consequences of defying societal expectations.

Furthermore, Chinese culture is steeply ingrained with beliefs in the supernatural. Chinese folklore is filled with stories of spirits and the afterlife, with a strong cultural understanding that the spirits of those who die under tragic or unfulfilled circumstances are prone to remain earthbound. This belief adds a layer of credibility to the tales of hauntings at the Opera House.

In addition, the architecture of the Huguan Huiguan Opera House adheres to principles of Feng Shui, the ancient Chinese practice of arranging spatial elements to harmonise energy or 'Qi'. Some Feng Shui theorists suggest that a disruption or imbalance of this energy could potentially invite or sustain paranormal activity. While the opera house's architecture is designed to optimise positive energy, the intense emotions associated with its history of performances could stir up the energy within its walls, potentially leading to the reported hauntings.

The high emotional intensity inherent to Chinese opera could also play a role in the Opera House's reputation for being haunted. Opera performances are a cathartic expression of human emotion, often invoking powerful responses from both performers and audiences. This energy, coupled with the tragic tales woven into the fabric of the building, might contribute to the heightened sense of paranormal activity.

The ghostly tales associated with the Huguan Huiguan Opera House are deeply rooted in its unique blend of Chinese folklore, history, and theatre. Through historical and cultural analysis, it becomes evident that the theatre's reported paranormal activity is not merely a product of superstition or overactive imaginations. Instead, it is a spectral echo of the opera house's rich past, a haunting harmony that adds an ethereal melody to the symphony of its existence.

A Cultural Overture in China

IN CHINESE SOCIETY, the role of opera extends far beyond entertainment. It is a vibrant tapestry of music, drama, and dance that is deeply intertwined with the nation's history, culture, and social constructs. Opera reflects societal norms, conveys moral lessons, and expresses deeply rooted emotions, making it a significant cultural institution. This cultural prominence of opera has a profound impact on how hauntings, particularly those connected to opera houses such as the Huguan Huiguan Opera House, are perceived and reported in Chinese society.

Opera in China is steeped in symbolism, with its narratives often exploring themes of honour, loyalty, love, and tragedy. As a result, opera houses are seen as repositories of emotional energy and historical significance. They are where stories of human passion and tragedy are told and retold, thereby potentially creating a rich emotional tapestry that might be conducive to hauntings. This view aligns with Chinese spiritual beliefs that places of intense emotional experience are likely to be inhabited by spirits.

The highly stylized and symbolic nature of Chinese opera also lends itself to the interpretation of ghostly encounters. Supernatural elements are integral to many traditional Chinese operas, with spirits, ghosts, and gods playing pivotal roles. This blurring of boundaries between the real and the supernatural in the realm of opera may encourage a greater openness towards experiences of the paranormal. It may also contribute to a sense of acceptance and even expectation of spectral presences in and around the opera house.

Chinese society also places significant emphasis on the concept of 'filial piety' - a Confucian virtue of respect for one's ancestors. This extends into a comprehensive belief system around spirits and the afterlife, including the idea that appeased ancestors offer protection and blessings, while disturbed spirits can cause misfortune. Consequently, reported hauntings might be treated with a degree of respect or reverence, seen not merely as supernatural anomalies but as indicators of unsettled spirits that need to be appeased.

Moreover, the cultural importance of opera can lead to frequent and vivid recounting of ghostly tales associated with the opera house. Storytelling is a cherished tradition in China, often serving to preserve history, impart moral lessons, and strengthen social bonds. Ghost stories related to the opera house can become part of this storytelling tradition, their frequent retelling reinforcing their presence in cultural memory and shaping the

perception of the opera house as a place where the spectral and
the real coexist.

The cultural importance of opera in Chinese society deeply
impacts how hauntings are perceived and reported. The themes
explored in opera, the societal beliefs regarding spirits, and the
tradition of storytelling all contribute to an environment where
reports of hauntings are not only expected but form part of the
opera house's cultural and historical narrative.

EDWARD TURNER

Chapter 8: The Palace Grand Theater in Dawson City, Canada

Apparitions from the Gold Rush Era

Situated in Dawson City, Yukon, the Palace Grand Theater is as much a monument to the area's gold rush history as it is a cultural institution. Its spectral stories, deeply intertwined with the region's mining past, resonate with the echoes of a bygone era. To understand the hauntings of the Palace Grand Theater, one must delve into the historical records, local lore, and personal accounts that have shaped its ghostly reputation over time.

Built during the Klondike Gold Rush in 1899 by Arizona Charlie Meadows, a showman and entrepreneur, the Palace Grand Theater was designed to bring entertainment and culture to a community fueled by the hopes of striking it rich. It soon became the heart of Dawson City's social scene, a place where miners and prospectors could momentarily escape the hardships of their daily lives.

However, the gold rush era was also a time of intense struggle and heartbreak, as many who journeyed to Dawson City with dreams of prosperity found only disappointment and death. These intense emotions—elation, despair, desperation—have left their mark on the theatre, leading to numerous accounts of spectral activity.

One of the most common apparitions is a woman in a flowing Victorian dress, often reported floating down the grand staircase or seen weeping in the balcony area. Local lore suggests that she is the spirit of a miner's wife, waiting eternally for her husband who perished in the mines. Her haunting presence is a stark reminder of the personal tragedies that often accompanied the quest for gold.

Another frequent sighting is of a man clad in miner's attire, believed to be Arizona Charlie himself. Interviewees have reported seeing him standing at the bar or sitting in the back of the theatre, watching performances with a pleased expression. Witnesses say that his apparition brings a sense of comfort rather than fear, a testament to his lifelong dedication to bringing joy to the mining community.

The local Yukon community holds a deep respect for these spirits, considering them an integral part of the theatre's history and charm. This perspective is rooted in indigenous beliefs about the interconnectedness of the living and the spirit world, reinforcing the acceptance of the theatre's hauntings.

To further investigate these phenomena, historical documents and old newspapers were consulted. They revealed numerous accounts of premature deaths and accidents during the gold rush era, providing a tragic context to the reported hauntings. Furthermore, many entries spoke of the theatre's vibrant atmosphere and crucial role in the community, explaining why the spirits might choose to linger in such a place.

The spectral stories surrounding the Palace Grand Theater reflect the region's vibrant and tumultuous mining history. Each sighting, each shiver down the spine, is a reminder of the individuals who lived, laughed, and grieved within its walls. The theatre's ghostly inhabitants are more than just spectral entities; they are the echoes of the past, continuing to play their roles in Dawson City's ongoing narrative.

Echoes in the Ethereal Veil

THE KLONDIKE GOLD RUSH was a transformative period in the Yukon region's history, shaping its societal fabric and leaving an indelible impact on its cultural heritage. The gold rush not only birthed a thriving community in Dawson City but also a trove of stories, including those that colour the haunting tales of the Palace Grand Theater. Understanding the historical context of the gold rush era offers valuable insights into the theatre's spectral narratives.

The discovery of gold in the Klondike region in 1896 triggered a massive influx of prospectors, driven by the allure of wealth and a chance to rewrite their destinies. Dawson City, at the heart of the gold rush, grew from a small settlement into a bustling metropolis almost overnight. The boomtown was filled with miners, entrepreneurs, adventurers, and dreamers from around the world, each carrying their own set of hopes, dreams, and fears.

This influx led to a unique societal dynamic, characterised by intense emotions and high stakes. Euphoria, desperation, triumph, and heartbreak were everyday emotions in Dawson

City. The dream of striking it rich was often met with harsh realities—brutal working conditions, scarce resources, and the ruthless competition of the goldfields. These conditions led to countless personal tragedies, often ending in premature death due to accidents, harsh weather conditions, or illness.

The Palace Grand Theater, established in this emotionally charged setting, was an oasis of culture and camaraderie for the hard-working miners. This combination of intense emotional energy and the theatre's role as a community hub may explain the high degree of spectral activity reported within its walls.

Historical events and societal changes of the gold rush era may have contributed to the formation of ghostly narratives at the theatre. The reported apparitions—of the miner's wife mourning her lost husband, and of Arizona Charlie himself—reflect typical figures of the era. Their stories encapsulate the dichotomy of the gold rush: the sorrow of those who lost loved ones to the harsh realities of mining, and the resilience of individuals like Arizona Charlie, who sought to infuse joy and culture into a challenging environment.

The psychological concept of place memory might also play a role in the theatre's hauntings. The idea is that locations where intense emotions or events have occurred can retain an imprint of that energy, which can manifest as paranormal activity. Given the emotional tumult of the gold rush era and the theatre's place within it, it's plausible that the Palace Grand Theater carries such imprints, contributing to its reputation as a haunted place.

GHOSTS OF THE STAGE: TEN HAUNTINGS AT THE THEATRE

The Klondike Gold Rush's intense historical events and their impact on the region and its society have undoubtedly influenced the ghostly narratives surrounding the Palace Grand Theater. The theatre's spectral tales are more than just intriguing supernatural anecdotes; they're echoes of a bygone era, interwoven with the fabric of Dawson City's rich and tumultuous history.

EDWARD TURNER

Chapter 9: The St. James Theatre in Wellington, New Zealand

Echoes of a Bygone Era

Perched in the heart of Wellington, New Zealand, the St. James Theatre is a beacon of cultural and historical significance. Constructed in 1912, it has withstood the test of time, witnessing wars, societal changes, and the evolution of the performing arts. But there is another dimension to the theatre's illustrious history that adds to its intrigue - the spectral whispers, phantom footsteps, and other paranormal phenomena that have given it a reputation as one of New Zealand's most haunted places.

One of the most frequently reported apparitions at the St. James Theatre is that of Yuri, a Russian performer who tragically fell to his death during a performance. Witnesses recount hearing the soft strains of music, a ghostly echo of a melody that resonates within the silent theatre long after the curtain has fallen. Some have reported seeing Yuri himself, wandering the backstage area, forever trapped in his last performance.

The theater's most chilling tales revolve around the infamous "Wailing Woman." Said to be the spirit of a performer who was rejected and heartbroken, her mournful cries can reportedly be heard echoing through the empty halls. Her specter, clad in an ethereal white dress, is often seen in the upper balconies, her sorrow permeating the air.

Phantom footsteps, another common phenomenon, reverberate through the theatre. Often associated with the spirit of a stagehand who died in an accident, these footsteps are an eerie reminder of the theatre's storied past.

To understand why these spectral occurrences might take place, one must delve into the history and cultural significance of the St. James Theatre. This theatre, like many others worldwide, has been a hub of human emotions—triumph, despair, passion, and grief—all of which are fundamental ingredients in the tapestry of theatre. The intensity of these emotions might leave a psychic imprint, manifesting as the reported spectral phenomena.

Moreover, the theatre's cultural significance might add to its ghostly allure. St. James Theatre has seen thousands of performances over the years, each leaving its unique imprint on the theatre's legacy. The emotional energy from these performances and the reactions they elicited could, according to some theories, contribute to the paranormal activity.

Furthermore, the theater's spectral narratives align with the broader cultural narrative of New Zealand's respect for spirits and the supernatural. Rooted in Maori spiritual beliefs, which perceive the spirit world and the physical world as intertwined, these narratives might influence how the paranormal events are interpreted by locals.

The spectral whispers, phantom footsteps, and other paranormal phenomena at the St. James Theatre are intrinsically linked with the theater's history and cultural significance. These reported experiences paint a vivid picture of a theater alive with the echoes of its past, a stage where the spectral performers are as much a part of the theater's story as their living counterparts.

The St. James Theatre's Hauntings and the Tides of Time

THE NARRATIVE OF THE St. James Theatre's hauntings is as deeply fascinating as it is mysterious. There appears to be a correlation between significant historical events and the periods of intense spectral activity reported at the theatre, hinting at an enthralling intersection of history and the supernatural.

During World War II, the theatre served as a refuge for servicemen and local citizens seeking solace from the turmoil outside its walls. It was during this era that the first accounts of spectral whispers and phantom footsteps began to surface. The intense emotional energy unleashed during wartime—a blend of anxiety, fear, hope, and sorrow—might have amplified the theatre's paranormal phenomena. The reports of spectral music, often described as melancholic yet soothing, could be the lingering echoes of performances aimed to provide comfort and escapism during these trying times.

In the late 1950s, when the threat of nuclear war hung heavy in the air, accounts of paranormal activity at the St. James Theatre surged. Notably, the "Wailing Woman" became a more frequent sight. Could her mournful wails be an ethereal echo of the public's fear and unease during this tense period? The parallel is undeniably intriguing.

In the 1980s, when the theatre faced demolition due to the growing popularity of television and cinema, stories of the apparition of Yuri, the Russian performer, increased. Was it coincidence or could Yuri's spirit have been stirred by the threat to his eternal stage?

Furthermore, the theatre underwent a significant restoration in the 1990s, during which paranormal incidents reportedly spiked. The refurbishment, although respectful to the theatre's original architecture, might have disrupted the spirits tied to the theatre, leading to an increase in their spectral activities.

It's also worth noting the connection to societal changes within New Zealand itself. For example, the resurgence of interest in Maori culture and spirituality from the 1980s onwards coincides with an increased acceptance and reporting of the paranormal phenomena at the St. James Theatre. The cultural shift towards acknowledging the supernatural may have led to a deeper understanding and acceptance of the theatre's spectral narratives.

The correlation between the reported hauntings at the St. James Theatre and significant historical events or societal changes underscores the theatre's symbiotic relationship with the world beyond its walls. As the tides of history ebb and flow, the theatre, with its spectral inhabitants, continues to play its part, creating an eternal echo of emotions, memories, and events that shape our collective consciousness.

Chapter 10: The Belasco Theater in New York, New York

The Grand Finale

As we draw the curtains on our tour of the world's most haunted theatres, there's no more fitting finale than the Belasco Theater. Nestled in the heart of Broadway, the theatre is steeped in history, bearing the echoes of countless performances and, if the reports are to be believed, the lingering presence of its former owner and his canine companion.

David Belasco, the theatre's founder, was a man of the theatre through and through. Known as the "Bishop of Broadway," his passion for the stage was legendary. According to numerous accounts, his spirit, along with that of his dog, continues to roam the theatre, watching over the performances from his private box and strolling along the balconies.

Witnesses have reported encounters with Belasco's apparition, distinguished by his clerical attire. His phantom, often accompanied by the faint smell of cigar smoke, is said to give approving nods to actors and occasionally offer spectral applause. The ghost of his dog, too, has reportedly been seen scampering through the corridors.

While sceptics might question the validity of these accounts, there is something compelling about the image of a theatre-loving spirit so bound to his creation that he refuses to leave, even in death. Belasco's spectral presence, seen as a sign of approval, has become a part of the theatre's lore, embraced by performers and theatregoers alike.

As we've journeyed through these haunted theatres, one thing has become abundantly clear: these spectral narratives, be they fact or fiction, play a crucial role in the theatre community. They serve as a link between the past and the present, between the tangible world of the living and the ethereal realm of the departed.

Each theatre's ghostly tale, whether it's of Yuri's eternal performance at the St. James Theatre or the tragic "Wailing Woman" of the Variety Theater, breathes life into its history, enriching its cultural heritage. The apparitions, spectral whispers, and phantom footsteps become as much a part of the theatre's story as the plays performed on its stage.

Moreover, these ghostly tales, steeped in history and mystery, add a layer of intrigue and fascination to the world of theatre, captivating audiences and performers alike. They serve as a testament to the emotive power of the theatre—the ability to elicit deep feelings that linger long after the actors have taken their bows.

So, as the spectral image of David Belasco applauds from his private box in the afterlife, we take our final bow. Our tour of haunted theatres concludes here, but the stage is ever set, the spectral lights always aglow. And who knows? The next time you're at the theatre, you might just catch a glimpse of a spectral performer out of the corner of your eye, silently mouthing their lines in an eternal performance.

The Geographic and Cultural Context of the Belasco Theater

THE BELASCO THEATER'S location on the famed "Great White Way," a segment of Broadway known for its concentration of professional theatre, is more than mere coincidence. This geographical and cultural context imbues the theatre with a unique aura, contributing to its storied reputation and its captivating spectral tales.

Broadway, particularly the segment known as the Great White Way, is synonymous with theatre. Since the late 19th century, it has been the heart and soul of American theatre, attracting talent from across the globe. The sheer concentration of theatres, each steeped in history, creates an environment ripe for legends and lore, spectral tales included.

The Belasco Theater is deeply interwoven into this vibrant tapestry of theatrical history. Built in 1907 by the theatre impresario David Belasco, it stands as a testament to the golden age of Broadway. Being in the epicentre of the theatre district, the Belasco Theater absorbed the energy and fervour of this dynamic environment, which could explain its reported paranormal activity.

Geographical context isn't the only contributing factor; the cultural context plays an equally vital role. The theatre district is not just a hub of performances; it's a melting pot of intense emotions - the thrill of a debut performance, the heartbreak of a poor review, the anticipation of opening night, the desolation of an empty stage. Such emotional intensity could, according to some theories, provide the ideal conditions for residual hauntings.

Furthermore, the Belasco Theater's ghost stories echo a larger cultural narrative. Tales of theatre ghosts are a time-honoured tradition on Broadway and have been part of theatre culture for centuries. They add an element of mystique and continuity, linking past performers with the present. In a way, these ghostly tales are an integral part of theatre tradition, bridging the gap between reality and the supernatural, much like theatre itself blurs the line between reality and fiction.

Moreover, the spirit of David Belasco resonates with the folklore of the theatre world. Ghosts are often seen as omens, and in the theatrical world, they're usually seen as good luck. Belasco's ghostly presence, rather than being a source of fear, is seen as a form of blessing, a spectral seal of approval from the theatre's founder himself.

The Belasco Theater's location on the Great White Way and its cultural context significantly contribute to its haunted reputation. The theatre stands as an ethereal monument to the unending passion for theatre, its spectral tales a testament to the enduring allure of Broadway, where the past and present converge in a dance as timeless as theatre itself.

Conclusion

Reflecting on our Ghostly Narratives

As we pull back the curtain on our spectral tour of the world's most haunted theatres, it's time to delve into an analysis of the shared themes and unique quirks that colour these ghost stories. More importantly, let's explore what these tales reveal about our perceptions of the supernatural, offering insights on how readers can thoughtfully engage with the paranormal while honouring the rich history and culture of these theatres.

Across the globe, from the New Amsterdam Theater in New York to the Huguang Huiguan Opera House in Beijing, there are striking similarities in the ghost stories that envelop these theatres. These spectral narratives are invariably tied to the theatre's history, often portraying characters from the past who left indelible marks on the stage or suffered tragic ends. For example, the Belasco Theater's owner, David Belasco, and the St. James Theatre's actor, Yuri, both continue their eternal performances even in death.

The prominence of these characters from the past underscores our collective desire for continuity, for maintaining a connection with those who came before us. In an increasingly transient world, these spectral tales offer a sense of timelessness, reinforcing the enduring nature of human emotions and experiences.

Despite these common threads, each theatre's ghostly tales have their unique inflections, shaped by their geographic and cultural contexts. For instance, the hauntings at the Palace Grand Theater are inextricably linked to the history of the Klondike Gold Rush, while the spectral narratives at the Huguang Huiguan Opera House are coloured by Chinese folklore and the cultural importance of opera in Chinese society. These variations demonstrate how our perception and interpretation of the supernatural are influenced by our cultural backgrounds and historical contexts.

Engaging with these ghostly tales allows us a unique opportunity to interact with the past, to learn about the history, culture, and traditions that have shaped these theatres. As we immerse ourselves in these spectral narratives, it's crucial to approach them with respect and an open mind. Remember, these stories are not just chilling tales meant to entertain or frighten; they're a part of the theatre's cultural heritage, a testament to its rich history.

As you sit in the audience, let your imagination wander to the times gone by. Picture David Belasco in his private box, offering spectral applause, or feel the energy of past performances that might still echo in the walls of the theatre. But always remember to honour the stories and the history they represent.

These ghostly tales are much more than supernatural phenomena; they're narratives that bridge the past and the present, that blend reality with the ethereal. They're an integral part of the theatre's history, reflecting our timeless fascination with the unknown and our enduring need for connection. So, as the curtain falls, let's take a bow to the ghosts of the stage, the eternal performers in the grand theatre of life.

Reflecting on the Supernatural

EMBARKING ON THIS JOURNEY of chronicling ten haunted theatres and their spectral narratives has been an enlightening experience. It has deepened my understanding of the supernatural, leaving me with a greater appreciation for the unknown and the unexplained. This chapter offers a moment of reflection, where I share my personal evolution and how these investigations have shaped my perception of the supernatural.

Initially, my view of the supernatural was ambiguous. Like many, I harboured both scepticism and curiosity, a delicate balance that often tipped one way or the other based on the circumstances. But as I dived into the research, journeyed through the spectral narratives, and connected the dots between history, culture, and paranormal phenomena, my perspective underwent a profound shift.

One key realisation that emerged from this journey is that these ghostly tales are not merely spine-chilling tales meant to thrill or terrify. Instead, they represent a compelling intersection of history, folklore, cultural context, and human emotions. Each spectral narrative is steeped in a theatre's history, its cultural backdrop, and carries a deeper meaning, often symbolising a desire for continuity, an attempt to bridge the past and the present.

While the investigations didn't necessarily convince me of the existence of ghosts in the traditional sense, they certainly led me to appreciate the cultural and psychological importance of such narratives. The ghost stories we explored seem to embody collective memories, emotional imprints, and historical echoes that resonate through time.

Belasco's eternal applause at his theatre or the tragic figure of the 'Wailing Woman' at the Variety Theater represent more than ghostly apparitions; they symbolise human passion, tragedy, love for art, and a connection to the past. This interpretation doesn't undermine the possibility of the supernatural but rather enriches our understanding of it.

In essence, these investigations have opened up a broader perspective for me, encouraging me to see beyond the surface of these haunting tales. They have reaffirmed my belief in the importance of narratives, how stories - even spectral ones - can deeply affect us, connect us, and give meaning to our experiences.

As I conclude this reflection, I find myself standing at the crossroads of the known and the unknown, of scepticism and belief, of the seen and the unseen. The exploration of these haunted theatres has not led to definitive answers but rather more questions, a sign of a journey well-travelled. And as we know, the allure of theatre, much like that of the supernatural, lies in its ability to captivate us, to make us question, wonder, and imagine.

So, as the final act of this book comes to a close, I invite you, dear reader, to take your own journey into the supernatural, into the fascinating realm of ghostly narratives. Listen to the echoes from the stage, to the whispers in the wings, and see what tales they tell you.

Don't miss out!

Visit the website below and you can sign up to receive emails whenever Edward Turner publishes a new book. There's no charge and no obligation.

https://books2read.com/r/B-A-SYIZ-VUKLC

BOOKS 2 READ

Connecting independent readers to independent writers.

Also by Edward Turner

Ghosts of Paris: Ten Haunted Places in the City of Love
Appalachian Nightmares: The Top 10 Creepy Creatures of the Mountains
Asia's Top Ten Cryptids: Legends, Sightings, and Theories
Beyond the Shadows: Unlocking the Mystery of Bigfoot
Evil Women in History: Uncovering the Gruesome Crimes of Ten Notorious Female Killers
Ghosts of London: Ten Haunted Places in The City
Ghosts of New York: Ten Haunted Places in The Big Apple
Ghosts of Oregon: The Top 10 Haunted Places You Must Visit
Ghosts of the Stage: Ten Hauntings at the Theatre
Missouri Nightmares: The Top 10 Chilling Legends
Mothman Unleashed: Into the Darkened Skies
North America's Top Ten Cryptids: Legends, Sightings, and Theories
Philly's Phantom Encounters: Exploring the City's Most Haunted Places
Secrets of the Deep: The Mystery of the Loch Ness Monster
Unsolved Mysteries: Delving into the Shadows of Infamous Murders and Enigmatic Killers
Unveiling the Shadows: A Journey into Financial Crimes and Scandals

About the Author

Edward Turner is a renowned author who specializes in exploring the realms of ghosts, the paranormal, and cryptids. With a captivating writing style and an insatiable curiosity for the unknown, Turner has garnered a dedicated following of readers who are captivated by his thrilling and eerie tales.

Born with an innate fascination for the supernatural, Turner has spent decades delving into the depths of paranormal phenomena, unearthing captivating stories and untangling mysteries that lie beyond the veil of the ordinary. His extensive research and meticulous attention to detail have earned him a reputation as a leading authority in the field.

Through his books, Turner expertly weaves together chilling accounts of encounters with ghosts, offering readers a glimpse into the ethereal world that coexists alongside our own. His ability to paint vivid portraits of spectral apparitions and convey the haunting atmosphere of haunted locations has made his works both spine-tingling and thought-provoking.

Turner's exploration of the paranormal doesn't stop at ghosts. He also dives into the fascinating world of cryptids—creatures that defy conventional explanation. His in-depth investigations into legendary creatures such as Bigfoot, the Loch Ness Monster, and the Chupacabra showcase his commitment to shedding light on these enigmatic beings.

With each page, Edward Turner's readers are drawn deeper into the enigmatic and unknown. His unique storytelling ability combined with his meticulous research has made him a sought-after author for those with an insatiable thirst for the supernatural. Whether delving into ghostly encounters or unraveling the mysteries of elusive cryptids, Turner's books offer a spine-chilling and immersive reading experience that leaves readers questioning the boundaries of our reality.

Edward Turner's works have earned critical acclaim and numerous accolades within the paranormal genre. He continues to explore the unexplained, captivating readers with his distinctive narrative style and unwavering dedication to unveiling the mysteries that lie hidden in the shadows.

9 798223 737377